PARENTING TEENS IN THIS TECH AGE:

Raising an amazing teenager against all odds

Frances E. Lowery

Table of content

Chapter 1: Raising teens in this technology world

Presently, for the maturity of teens, their virtual world is an extension of their real life. Media and digital bias are fast becoming an essential part of their world. They are growing up digitally. So, it's vital to help them learn the generality of the right digital use and parents play an important part in conducting this education.
It can be great, if these digital biases are used fairly and properly. As parents, we need to show how to make a stable balance between digital and real- world relations. Studies show that face- to- face time spent with family, buddies, and instructors play an important part in promoting teens' learning and healthy development. And hence, striking the right balance becomes important.

How to save your teen from getting loss in media and technology sluice

1) Talk to Your Teens Regularly
There is no swish time to start a discussion with your teens about their digital life. One most important thing that you can do as a

parent is to have regular exchanges about your teen's digital life. Try to understand how they are using the internet and how they would like to be supported. It will help you to be more set to help them deal with safety issues. This will also cover them from unwanted trolling and stalking.

You can indeed establish a respectable family internet operation contract to help your teens learn how to swish and use the internet to enhance their lives online. Always flashback, these days, teens spend nearly more than a third of their day on social media or other online exertion. So, it's important that as parents, we take the time to give proper motherly guidance to help our teens navigate the digital world.

2) Proactively Track and Limit Access

As per the disquisition done by the Pew Research Center, 39 of surveyed parents had used motherly controls or other technological tools to block certain websites and apps. Always flashback, do not put strict restrictions on teens. Differently, they are more likely to engage in unsafe online behavior. Teenagers generally know the loopholes. So, your tech-smart teen can disable babes or clean browsing history. They easily find a way to pierce the content they want to. So, if you put further pressure on them, they will try to hide their online behavior.

To protect your teen from serious online behavior, you can set up a home router with motherly controls, you can establish non-negotiable electronic operation rules, and can limit their screen time.

You can bridge the gap between safety and freedom by setting up a fair system for how teens use their bias and how to swish cover their behavior while maintaining a sense of liberty. You shouldn't toss your teen a device without giving them any knowledge about how to correctly use it.

3) Educate Your Teen the Three Ws.

Before your teen posts anything on social media, encourage them to spot check and ask themselves WHY, WHO, and WHAT. Who is your followership (Would it be good enough if your father or grandmother saw this)? What is the communication you are trying to shoot with this social media post and is it in line with your core values? Why are you posting this? If this image/ communication/ video/ Audio was publically accredited to you, how would you feel?

4) Educate Them On Healthy managing Strategies
As a mortal being, mood change is completely normal. But, generally, teenagers take their passions to social media. So, parents should help teens in erecting awareness and chancing healthy managing strategies to tone- regulate and reduce the intensity of a particular situation before posting anything online. Teenagers generally do not think about long-term consequences. And, this can be a form for tragedy. So, help your teens to plant a seed of reflection in advance. It can make a big difference.
5) Practise What You Preach
Make sure you also change, If you want your teen to change. Flashback, to the adage, Do as I say, not as I do. So, prioritize offline connections. Also as parents, you should turn off your bias and turn towards them, if you want your teens to turn into you. Prefer face-to- face exchanges with your children and hear them precisely and keenly when they are talking to you. Set limits on your teens' technology use, emphasize real- life relations and put in practice what you preach. Stop checking your mobile constantly when a teen is talking to you. By doing so, you may be part- modeling the behavior you want your teen to avoid. As a parent, you can't change the world that your children find themselves in, but surely, you can help them navigate it

Teens and technology

When it comes to teens and technology, it's a whole new world moment, literally an online bone. Technology has converted what it means to be a teenager. It permeates every part of their lives from academe to home and has completely changed the dynamics of their connections and communication. Trying to parent our tweens and teens with all these biases, apps and social media is challenging, especially considering half the time it feels like they know far further than we do(okay perhaps all the time).
The turn it off battles, figuring out if and how we should cover our teens' tech use and training them to be safe and wise about their online exertion is enough to make multitudinous parents crazy. But the worst part of it all is the solicitude. We worry about what our

teens and tweens are doing, who they are meeting and what they might be seeing online. It does not always matter to us until too late how a smartphone can open our teenagers up to so many implicit risks.

Teens and social media

There is a long list of the ways technology can harm our tweens and teens, but the goods of social media on teens is the most concerning. As the rates of self- murder, depression and anxiety are growing at intimidating rates among tweens and teens, much of the validation points to smart phones and in particular access to social media spots. Social media powers the insecurity of our adolescents at a time when they are most vulnerable. It creates a no way ending feedback circle that is constantly filled with unrealistic images, openings for comparison and a need for constant declaration.

Parents are strongly advised about allowing tweens access to social networking spots. The spots themselves indeed suggest that 13 should be the minimum age for joining. By high academy, allowing some social media becomes more reasonable. Our teens do need to learn how to manage social media, because it will be an ineluctable part of their adult experience. Further they begin with our guidance.

The cons of tech use

We also need to keep in mind, not all tech is bad. There are multitudinous ways that technology can be salutary to our tweens and teens. Our immature people can explore the world in ways no way accessible to former generations. They can get answers to all their most burning questions with a simple Google quest, they can learn to dive just about any task by watching a YouTube video and also can indeed go to academe nearly.

Plus, while absolutely there are some apps that aren't a good idea for teens, there are tons of other teen apps that can help our tweens and teens in numerous areas. There are practice apps, organizational apps and indeed apps to help them prepare for the SAT and ACT.

Raising digital smart teens

At the end of the day, parenting tweens and teens in the moment's technology world don't mean we have to be tech experts. What we need to raise digitally smart tweens and teens is to stop viewing the online world as a commodity fully foreign.

Numerous parenting strategies we apply to their offline lives, also apply online. It's about paying attention, staying tuned in, and setting age-applicable rules and boundaries. It's also about administering consequences and always flashing back that technology is an honor, not a right.

Also, we shouldn't be hysterical to ask our tweens and teens for help when it comes to what we may not know about the bottommost tech contraptions and trends. Most of the time they'll be happy to show off their moxie and it can indeed be a great way to connect with our tweens and teens. No one cares further about your child's well-being and success than you do. In a moment's digital-fuelled times, that means guiding him or her not just in the real world but in the always-on virtual one as well. Educate your children to use technology healthily and pick up the chops and habits that will make them successful digital citizens. From 2- time- histories who feel to understand the iPad better than you to teenagers who need some (but not too important) freedom, will walk you through how to make technology work for your family at each stage of the trip

Do this if you want to maintain tech harmony at home

Numerous introductory parenting guidelines will help you establish ground rules and maintain tech harmony at home.
1. Aim for Balance

It's clear that technology is also to stay and the world is getting only more digitally driven. In multitudinous ways, that's a good thing. Technology can be empowering for youths of all ages, with tools that help children learn in fun and engaging ways, express their creativity and stay connected to others. Children who are tech-moxie will also be more set for a pool that will be generally digital. At the same time, parents naturally worry about their youths piercing unhappy content online, the impact of two important screen time on healthy development, and their children getting tethered to technology.

As with utmost situations, a balanced approach to these new challenges works best." The most important step is to establish a balanced or sustainable relationship with tech," says the social psychologist Adam Alter, author of contagious The Rise of Addictive Technology and the Business of Keeping Us Hooked. You can liken it to aiming for a healthy diet, Dr. Alter explains" progressed youths understand the generality of balance privately-- they know that It's important to eat healthy foods alongside delicacy and the same is true of the empty calories' that come from spending too important time passively peering at defenses. There's time for defenses, but not at the expense of time for physical exertion and connecting with real people in real-time."

Some effects to keep in mind as you try to strike this delicate balance:

There's no single form for success, but you'll know it when you see it. Balance for your family will look different than it will for your neighbor because every family is unique and parenting styles and values vary. In general, still, if your family can reap the benefits of technology without feeling multitudinous about the dangerous goods and you feel confident in how your children are using technology, you've probably set up a balance.

Watch for the warning signs of unhealthy tech operation. The psychologist Jon Lasser, who wrote" Tech Generation Raising Balanced youths in a Hyper-Connected World," says parents should note when youths complain that they're jaded or unhappy when they don't have access to technology, explosions or harsh resistance when you set screen time limits. Screen time interferes with sleep, academy, and face-to-face communication.

Be set to readdress this content again and again. As your children grow, so will their involvement with technology. Also, it's delicate to predict what the digital world will look like indeed just numerous times from now. Your description of healthy and unhealthy tech operations will need regular updates.

Some tips to estimate the quality of your children's digital relations (which you should do regularly): Are they penetrating age-applicable content? Are the apps they use interactive and study-provoking rather than unresisting? Not all screen time is equal. Going back to the food analogy, 100 calories from a doughnut isn't the same as 100 calories from a salad; an hour watching YouTube videos is not the same as an hour spent in a digital art program.

Are the sequestration settings for aged children's social media and other online accounts set to circumscribe what non-natives can see and who can communicate with your children? Still set screen time limits to balance online and offline conditioning. Although quality is most important, you will presumably still want to set some screen time limits for your family to save time for conditioning beyond defenses and tech. While the debate on exactly how numerous hours kiddies can spend on their defenses before it becomes unhealthy enthusiasm, you can draw firm lines for tech-free times, similar as during regale, in the auto, or on academy nights.

2. Be a part Model

Technology's infectious pull draws in parents as much as it does kiddies. We check our phones every hour, log late hours working or probing the internet on our laptops, binge-watch our favorite shows, and indeed engage in dangerous" distracted walking." Children are likely to not only copy our behavior, but they also feel like they've to contend with a bias for our attention. Nearly half of parents in one study reported technology snooping with relations with their child three or further times on a typical day.

Google and Apple are starting to address this growing concern about tech taking over our lives by adding new phone features similar to time limits for specific apps(for Android) and statistics on time spent on the bias(for iOS). While digital tools can help us check inordinate contrivance operation, rehearsing and demonstrating the aware use of technology ourselves will be the stylish way to educate children on the critical skill of freeing. Set boundaries for work time and family time. Many crucial times to stay unplugged include:When picking up or dropping children at the academy, as this is a transitional time for them.After coming home from work, that is time to reconnect with your family. During meals, including when dining out. During jaunts like passages to the demesne or zoo, or recesses when the focus is on family time.

Know when you are busy and need to be plugged in and when you don't. Frequently, it feels like there is work or social urgency and you have to take that call, respond to a communication, or check your dispatch — but when you think about it, it could stay until after you've finished that movie or game with your child.

Use the media the way you want your children to. Follow common-sense rules around tech like no way texting while driving and avoiding oversharing on social media. By rehearsing what you sermonize rather than the hypocritical " do as I say not what I do" approach, you emulate the habits you want your children to pick up and show them that there are times for using technology and times when we should be present in the real world.

3. Make Tech a Family Affair

Your family likely discusses important opinions that affect the group day-to-day, similar to who is responsible for doing the dishes and where you should go for your coming holiday. Technology use should take the same type of planning, so everyone's on board with the same prospects.

Set rules as a family. When you set limits with children, Dr. Lasser says, kiddies can start learning how to tone-regulate and know when screen time is snooping too important for the rest of their lives. As a perk, he adds" kiddies are also less likely to compromise at limits if they have a part in creating and establishing them." You can produce a family media use plan at the American Academy of Pediatrics website.

Be involved with your child's tech experiences. Playing or watching alongside your children offers several benefits. You will be suitable to vet the content they're penetrating, the child will learn further from the exertion through your interaction, and you will bond through the participating experience. However, let them educate you

— it's confidence- supporter for them and important for you to keep up with the new experiences they are having If your children feel to be light times ahead in tech with you. This might mean sitting through dizzying Mine craft builds, Fortnight games, or learning teen-speak, but at least you will witness the virtual world together.

Confirm your approach to each child. As with other areas of parenthood, what works for one child will not inescapably work for another, depending on their periods, personalities, and needs. Your 10- time-old might be more careful about not playing unhappy games or keeping your computer free of contagions than your 12- time-old. Your 12- time-old might not want a phone indeed though her musketeers all have one.

Guideline for age ranges on the use of tech

Babies Under 2

They are unexpectedly complete at tapping and swiping, but keep the phone and tablet down as important as possible(exchanges with Grandma are okay).One second you are holding your cooing, happy baby and the coming she's bawling in the eatery. Hand over a smartphone, however, and all is well again. It's no wonder parents frequently resort to electronic bias to distract. With their endless array of dazing apps and cartoons on YouTube, widgets snare babies' attention.

The problem is that a child's brain grows fastest in the first three times of life, which makes this period the most critical one. For lingual, emotional, social, and motor chops development. Being suitable to witness the real world with all of her senses and through live commerce with others will be far more salutary to a baby than interacting with a screen. A picture of a ball, indeed if it bounces and makes a sound on the screen, is not as rich an experience as playing with a factual ball.

It's O.K. to introduce your children to technology, but it should be a bitsy chance for their time at this age and immaculately to participate with you since babies are social learners. The maturity of their awake time should be spent doing what babies do stylishly, absorbing everything around them and developing their big smarts.

 For Any Screen Time, Focus on Quality

The jury's still out on the long-standing debate of" How important is screen time?" In 2016, the American Academy of Pediatrics (AAP) revised its former recommendation of no screen time for children under 2. The new guidelines were broadened a bit, with recommendations for only videotape drooling for children under 18 months, co-watching high-quality programs, similar to the classic Sesame Street or Wonder faves! for children periods 18 to 24 months, one hour a day of screen time for children periods 2 to 5 times, and" harmonious limits" on screen time for children periods 6 and over.

 A study from Oxford University published in December 2017 set up no harmonious correlation between parents who followed the A.A.P. screen time guidelines and youthful children's well-being. That study's lead author, Dr. Andrew Pryzbylski, said in a statement," If anything, our findings suggest the broader family environment, how parents set rules about digital screen time, and if they are laboriously engaged in exploring the digital world together, are more important than the raw screen time."

 Some tips for finding the right balance for your baby

 Limit tech operation to the bare minimum. The A.A.P. recommends limiting tech use to videotape drooling — for illustration with a traveling parent or cousins who are far down. The one-to-one exchanges, indeed on screen, can help babies as they develop critical language chops.

 Skip the" educational" videos. Products like Baby Einstein DVDs and other videos retailed as helping babies' smarts grow have been linked to experimental issues, sleep problems, and detainments in learning essential chops like vocabulary. Parents are busier than ever, with work,meals to make, ménage chores, and taking care of other family members. Still, rather than using technology as an electronic anodyne or sitter, if you are unfit to tend to the baby for a moment, give the baby toys or books that will help her use all her senses. When using a tablet or phone with your baby, talk, read, sing or play with them to nourish their brain development. Interactive books can be engaging, as can musical apps or ones that educate

children to fete letters, figures, colors, and shapes. (Stylish kiddies Apps offer a curated list.)
Protect your devices
 While too important technology exposure can be dangerous for your baby, your baby can also be dangerous to your technology. The stylish protection is forestallments. Lock down your devices so kiddies cannot accidentally make in-app purchases or destroy your device. Lock down your phone and tablet with defensive cases that have thick padding, are easy to clean and are easy for small hands to hold. Amazon offers a case for its Fire tablet, while there are multitudinous options for iPad possessors.
 Set up maternal controls on your bias. For Android, use the Family Link app to manage apps and set screen time limits. For iOS, go to Settings> General> Restrictions to limit apps and features.
 Once your child is old enough to understand introductory instructions, start tutoring how to take care of these biases, with rules like" Do not eat or drink around the computer, Do not leave the iPad on the bottom, Your phone isn't a coaster. And when they're aged, consider when its applicable to ask them to help pay for any damage that results when they disregard your warning

Toddlers and Preschoolers (2- 5 Times)

 Play, watch and browse together — while sculpturing out further tech-free time.
 Once your child is running about and eager to learn all the effects, it will bc hard to keep electronic bias down. A check by Erikson Institute showed that 85 percent of parents allow their children under age 6 to use technology at home and 86 percent of parents surveyed said they set up benefits for their youthful children's tech exercises, including knowledge, academy readiness, and academy success. While there are further apps and widgets than ever ahead explicitly designed for toddlers, you will still want to make tech a small slice of their larger literacy and conditioning pie.
Make Tech Time Bonding Time
 At this age, children are learning pre-social behavior. Sharing, helping, giving, and serving other people. It's the age when kids

learn to give and take. Technology can help with this experimental stage when you play with them, taking turns and exploring a game or digital book or videotape together. Now(and, actually, at every other age), children want your concentrated attention — indeed when their focus seems to be substantially directed at a screen.

Choosing Games and Apps

 You'll want to do this for your youths in any age group, but as soon as possible, get into the habit of checking age conditions for digital content. Stephen Balkam, the author and C.E.O. of the Family Online Safety Institute, a non profit that represents members analogous to Amazon and Verizon with the end of making the online world safer for children and families, recommends checking the International Age Rating Coalition (IARC) conditions versus app store conditions. Google, Microsoft, Nintendo, and numerous other major tech companies use IARC conditions when producing user content and these conditions are linked to public age standing systems.

 Some toddler-friendly apps include Kiddie, Google's visual quest machine for youths, and Kidoz, a curated collection of children's apps andcontent.CommonSenseMedia.org offers reviews of apps and games sorted by age group. It's important to keep in mind that age recommendations in app stores and spots like YouTube haven't always been accurate, still(some providers go out of their way to insinuate the registries with disturbing content masquerading as child-friendly) so the swish expedient is to vet the content your youths are exposed to yourself. Establish rules for when the family should not be on their bias, analogous as two hours before bedtime and during mess times. Also, set up screen-free zones in your home. For illustration, mobile devices, computers, and TVs are not allowed in the dining room or bedrooms. Establish rules like these — that everyone in the family follows — makes sure everyone gets tech breaks and family time

For Young Children (6- 12 years)

Now is the time to set up and support healthy tech habits. Children at this academy age position will presumably be using technology on a quotidian base. As they still look to you for guidance, this is a vital time to establish and support the applicable use of technology and the benefits your family can gain from it.

Set Up Child Accounts

Youths in this age range may need to use a computer for practice. The erected- motherly controls in Windows (called Microsoft Family) and macOS(called motherly Controls in system preferences) can help you set time limits and also limit apps and web operations. As important as you might try to train them, there will be accidents. A laptop dropped on the floor, milk revealed on the keyboard, or defenses broken from mysterious" I didn't do that!" causes. The swish protection is to designate certain biases specifically for children to use (maybe your old ones; if you have a charge-critical computer or tablet that you use for work, keep your youths off it.

Chrome books are affordable laptops, so they might be a good choice for immature children. And if you keep devices in a central position, analogous to a family room, you'll be better suited to cover your youths' tech operation and be more engaged with them when they go online.

Encourage Creativity:

Technology has a lot to offer children, but the apps you choose to expose your youths to make a difference. However, If your child is a tinkerer and likes to make things. You could try Osmo, which merges real-world objects with digital ones on the iPad for a further tactile knowledge experience. Scratch, developed by M.I.T., teaches children logic through creating stories, robustness, and games.Try family-friendly active video games for the Wii, Playstation, or Xbox, analogous to Wipe out produce & Crash.

Sequestration and Security Best Practices:

Start the safety discussion beforehand and speak about it constantly. Remind youths that what goes online stays online and that they should in no way partake tête- à- tête identifiable or sensitive information." It may not be realistic for parents to become experts on every new app that becomes popular," Mr. Balkam says," but by establishing an open discussion with their child from the launch, they can help them stay safe. Children who are used to talking about what they do online are more likely to tell someone if they are worried or upset by a commodity that happens in their digital life."Online safety cards for youths' technology can help you set up the ground rules for your children when you give them a new device.

Watch Out for Cyber bullying

Bullying — both online and offline — becomes an implicit issue for children once they're in grade academe." The disquisition on this content generally shows that youths' online lives image their offline lives," says Lisa Damour, author of" Untangled Guiding Teenage Girls Through the Seven Transitions into Adulthood." Her general guidance for parents to give their youths: Do not be an unresisting bystander if you witness bullying, online or in real life, Alert a grown-up.Stand up to the bully on behalf of the victim. Go out of your way to support the victim, analogous to including the person in your exertion or checking in to see they are Okay.

Phone usage

At this age, your youths might be clamoring for a phone of their own, since presumably some of their buddies have them. According to Nielsen disquisition, the most predominant age when youths get a phone with a service plan is 10, followed by 8, and also 9 and 11(tied for third). Most parents give their children phones so they can easily get in touch or track youths' positions for safety reasons.But just because all the other youths have a phone doesn't mean your child is ready for one. Things you'll want to consider before buying them phones: Are they responsible for their effects? Will they follow your rules around phone use? Can they be trusted to use text, prints, and video responsibly?

You'll need to check your child's maturity position also and consider your family's values. For illustration, if a phone is demanded safety reasons, a" dumb phone"(flashback those?) or burner phone might be a result. There's no magic age number, but utmost experts recommend staying as long as possible to delay youths' exposure to online bullies, child bloodsuckers, sexing, and the distractions of social media.

For Teens (13- 18 Times)

Children at this age want further freedom and insulation, but you still need to make sure they're safe. Stay connected while maintaining that trust. Teens will want further independence, and that includes using their bias without you prying into their social lives. You might move from strict monitoring to mentoring your teen to use tech responsibly.

Set Rules

You should set rules on phone and device operation (if you haven't formerly).

" It's inoperable for parents to try to supervise everything teenagers do online," Dr. Damour says," but it's possible to use periodic monitoring to get a sense of how well an immature person is handling the freedom of having access to digital technology. From there, parents can decide how snappily they can expand their tweens/ teen's freedoms." A phone contract can help establish the guidelines your teen should have in mind when he or she's online. Some-debatable rules might include: No texting while driving, No sharing unhappy prints or videos, Always texting you when arriving at or leaving a friend's house.

Best Practices on the use of tech by adolescence

Educate social media and critical thinking best practices. Once teens have a phone, they'll be using it primarily as a social tool, so support the positive aspects of that while advising them of the troubles (e.g., commodity online can follow you through life). And affirm whenever possible that your teen's tone-worth shouldn't be tied to likes or shares. This is also the time to bathe how marketing dispatches can be used to manipulate people and to encourage your teen to fact-check rumors and be skeptical of anything they come across online.Follow your youths on social media, so you can see what they're over to periodically. Make this a non-negotiable rule —

indeed if your youths discomfit at it." Staying involved and not overreacting to every post tends to be a more subtle form of supervision that teens may tolerate indeed as they get aged and want further insulation," Mr.Balkam advises.

Establish Trust

   At this delicate stage, you'll need to balance respect for your youths' need for insulation while also icing they're safe. Some ideas for ground rules You won't hear on phone exchanges or check their emails unless you suspect a commodity is wrong. In return, they will hand over their phone or online account login any time they want to review their exertion. This lets teens know that you reserve the right to look out for them, without destroying trust if you were to cover them without letting them know you were doing that.

The technology and social media researcher Danah Boyd offers a smart strategy for establishing trust with your children while having access to their online accounts as demanded" Parents ask children to put watchwords into a piggy bank that must be broken for the paper with the word to be reacquired. analogous parents constantly explain that they don't want to pierce their teen's accounts, but they want to have the capability to do so in case of emergency.' A piggy bank allows a social contract to take a physical form."

Steer Them into Productivity

Channel teens' tech interests into productive purposes. Digital knowledge is a skill increasingly in demand and technology can offer implausible creative and academic opportunities. However, see if there are classes on programming, and digital design, If your child is interested. There are free programming classes around the world, and Microsoft and Apple give pleasurable computer-predicated shops in their stores, generally in the summer.

Avoiding Tech Dependence

There are two major early warning signs you should look out for to check if your child has an unhealthy relationship with technology, Dr. Alter says. One is behavioral and the other emotional."On the behavioral front, it's important to fend when defenses are taking up such an important time that there's no time left for playing offline, doing physical exercise, and spending time face- to face with other people.

On the emotional front, it's important to fete when youths substantiate negative passions after screen time because they're feeling bullied, ostracized, or more generally unhappy as a result of their online relations. That may be after they spend time on social networks, communicating by text, or when they play a multiplayer part- playing games with a social element." Be on the lookout if your child replaces offline conditioning he used to enjoy with farther screen time, if sleep begins to suffer due to late-night tech operation, and if in-person relations (like having family feasts) get commandeered by bias. As with utmost parenting motifs, constant, open communication is pivotal to helping your family reap the benefits of technology without passing on too many of the negative effects.

Chapter 2: Nonchalance in teens

Every generation has its view about the different goods that are in society. Nonchalance is one issue that seems to be current in nearly all teenagers in the moment's society I don't watch is the universal teen maxim". This station is giving the aged generations a run for their capitalism because they do not know how to go about handling it or why the teens indeed display this station.
Teenagers are always changing because they are going through puberty from the ages of 0 – to 18. Everything they do will not be fully understood and this can be proven with disquisition. Teenagers are characterized by their serious behavior. Teens partake in dumb exertion that they are upon at the moment, It's true, teens are impulsive, but they are also vulnerable and dynamic. This vulnerability is what ultimately leads a teen to display an incurious station. They are using it as a way to hide how they truly feel because they do not want to be open to an attack in utmost cases, your child deploys a nonchalant attitude because she wants to show defiance as a defense medium … you discipline as you wish and she undermines you by acting as if she does not watch. Portraying this I don't watch attitude is the only way the teen feels that they can

defend themselves because they don't want to give their authority figure the benefit of the mistrustfulness by expressing how they truly feel It's mortal nature to project passions of guilt, responsibility and negativity away, replacing those passions with insouciance Teens insouciance is the mask that conceals the true passions and opinions teenagers are too spooked to express due to feeling embarrassed or because they do not want to come off as being weak.

 Weakness is one reason this insouciance mask is worn. They want to appear in control and strong at all times because it shows that they aren't naive little kiddies presently; they're aged and able to make their own opinions. It's just like a poker face. The person is calm and collected on the outside, but on the inside, the person is sweating pellets because everything is going upward or about to go upward for them. No teen wants their life to be controlled like a poppet by their parents. As your child begins to play her agency and form habits, bents, and interests, she may use an incurious station to assert her own opinions. Most parents fail to fete that they're their person and just a reflection of you. Teenagers aren't their parents, so parents should stop trying to make opinions that make only themselves happy and not their teens. Teens aspire to be different from their parents in life, so making opinions for them is only portraying how parents want their children to be like them, or in some cases be like them. This is seen with parents who try to live vicariously through their children. Parents try to live a non age life they couldn't fulfill through their teen, but this only calls for the teen to be unhappier. This is when the teen will portray the I do not watch attitude because they know that anyhow of what they tell their parents they will not consider their opinions.

 Opinions shape teenagers' lives further than people realize although it's unanimously known that youthful people can't make good opinions. This is viewed by teens because they believe every decision they make is a good one, so when a teen has a chance to make their own opinions it's a big deal to them. Teens frequently have an apathetic or dismissive station about anything other than what they want to do Teenagers want to engage in effects on their own because during non age we're developing our opinion on the world and our environment they don't want to live a life grounded off someone else view of the world because this will eventually not bring them happiness. Teens take further pitfalls not because they don't understand the troubles but because they weigh price versus threat differently.

Teens don't watch about the pitfalls they take because the price that ensues brings them happiness. This means that" adolescents are less likely to modify their dangerous or unhappy actions. Because they know that these actions are linked to a price that will put a smile on their face. Danger doesn't count when the price brings a teen happiness. This is because " the area of the brain that controls logic and helps us suppose before we act develops later", so teens aren't completely responsible for this incurious view towards dangerous or perilous actions. Also, the fact that they're deciding on their own makes them indeed happier; it's only when the life a teen wants to live conflicts with the life their parents want them to live does an incurious station present itself. In this case" the incurious and stoic wall that the teen puts up in front of you means they're generally dealing with hurt, disappointment, fear, and anger internally. Saying I do not watch on the outside, but emotionally distraught on the inside is what's taking place.

This strange behavior is what eventually sets teenagers apart from grown-ups. Teenagers are still learning to use their brain's new networks. This means that they're prone to display reckless actions, unstable feelings, and detachment to the utmost effects they encounter in life because" their conduct is guided more by the amygdala and lower by the anterior cortex". This detachment from reality is what eventually proves to be a teen's worst adversary. The I don't care attitude begins to take over them, and they begin to suppose everything will just fall in place in their lives with no trouble on their end. The peril is that teens use that fantasy to justify their poor station around their liabilities.

This annuity brought on by not minding prompts parents to take action which will only lead to an increase in insouciance among teenagers. When authority numbers have a say-so in what's taking place, The adolescent statement" I don't watch" is an attempt to ease the heartbreak over maternal blessing ... to assert further independence and develop further individuality. This means that teens do watch what their parents are telling them, but because they want to be their person, they go against whatever is stated. This intransigence is brought about because the teens won't settle for anything other than what they want. They're motivated to achieve what they want. And won't give up fluently when defied, rejected or refused". Intransigence plays a pivotal part in the stations seen among teenagers in moment's society, but this intransigence can eventually work in their favor when it comes time for a result to this problem. Hence By giving them an overall thing of success to work towards, and constantly creating new ways to keep them engaged the incurious station will sluggishly disappear. However, they will watch more and put further trouble towards achieving this happiness, If the provocation/ alleviation directly relates to a teen's happiness. They will no longer watch about how numerous times they fail at something; they will continue to try to achieve success because they know it'll get them near to their thing of happiness. They will also no longer be worn out or do something because they were forced to do it. The decision to pursue what makes them happy is fully theirs, so nonchalance will no longer be used as a defense mechanism because the teens are happy and don't feel vulnerable.

How to curb nonchalance in teens

Teens with literacy and attention issues may be more likely to engage in parlous actions, similar to alcohol and medicine abuse or vulnerable coitus. These suggestions may make your teen less likely to do so.

1. Make rules and stick to them

Rather than giving your teen more freedom just because he's aged, it may be good to have your teen show he's responsible enough for his freedom. You can do that by making rules and sticking to them. Don't make rules up on the spot. Bandy rules ahead of time with your teen so he easily understands them. Your curfew is 1000 on Friday night. However, shoot me a textbook communication, if you're going to be any later than that. However, you habituate be suitable to play videotape games for a week, If that does happen. Then stick to it.

2. Let your teen make opinions.

Setting rules for your teen is important. It's also good to start letting him make some opinions. He'll need to make opinions once he becomes a grown-up, so this can be practiced. However, you may not want to automatically say no, for illustration, If your teen comes home and says he wants to quit the football platoon. Talking to him about why he wants to quit might be a better option. You could ask him if he's willing to give it another month before he quits. This can help your teen understand that it's good to suppose through opinions.

3. Give structure and routine.

Teens who spend a lot of time unsupervised may be more likely to get into dangerous situations. And teens who feel close to their families are less likely to engage in parlous behaviors. However, set up a time formerly a week when your family has regale or does a delightful spin together, If possible. You can also make structure into your child's schedule. You can hang out with Tommy after the academy, but I'd like you back by 400 to start homework. Routines, like a wake- up and lights-out times, can also help.

4. Get to know your teen's musketeers.

Who does your teen spend time with? Teenagers tend to get a lot of their beliefs from parents and musketeers. Encourage your teen to invite musketeers over so you can meet them. You could also get to know their parents. However, or you suspect they are, you may want to steer your teen to healthier musketeers by having him subscribe up for adulterous conditioning he likes If your teen's musketeers are engaging in parlous actions. Keeping your child busy in a safe, structured terrain may help him from making bad choices.

5. Help your teen find a tutor.

It's normal for teens to start pulling down on their parents. But you may also want to introduce your teen to other grown-ups and aged kiddies who can be a good influence on him. A tutor is a role model your teen can look up to, similar to a relative, sports or music trainer, or an aged child with literacy and attention issues. Having a tutor can make a teen less likely to abuse alcohol and medicines.

6. Let your teen know you watch him.

Teens might occasionally feel like they can't do anything right — especially those with literacy and attention issues. Let your teen know you watch him and that he can come to you with problems. This could make him less likely to engage in parlous behavior than a teen who feels unconnected. Give leverages and give a shoulder to cry on when he has a bad day. Praise him for the effects he's doing well, and admit his sweats. I know English class is tough this time. I'm proud of you for keeping up with the reading.

Discourteous behavior

Discourteous behavior is a common part of teenage development. This phase generally passes. You can avoid or handle discourteousness with positive communication, strong connections, and clear family rules. It's stylish to avoid arguing, being protective, and troubling. Discourteousness is a common part of teenage development, although not all teenagers are rude or discourteous. It happens incompletely because your child is developing, expressing, and testing independent ideas and values, so there'll be times when you differ. Developing independence is a crucial part of growing up. It's a good sign that your child is trying to take further responsibility. But your child is also still learning how to handle disagreement and differing opinions appropriately.

Also, your child is trying to balance their need for sequestration with your need to stay connected and show you watch. So occasionally you might get a rude or discourteous response because your child feels you're too interested in their life or conditioning.

Your child's moods can change snappily too. Because of the way teenage smarts develop, your child can't always handle changing passions and responses to every day or unanticipated effects and this can occasionally lead to over-sensitivity, which in turn can lead to crotchetiness or rudeness. Teenage brain development can also affect your child's capability to empathize and understand other people's perspectives, including yours.

Occasionally discourteous behavior might be a sign that your child is feeling stressed out or feeling anxious. Teenagers are also starting to suppose and feel more deeply about the effects. Some youthful people feel to have a disagreeing and radical view on everything, and they might question preliminarily held beliefs. This shift to deeper thinking is a normal part of development too. And occasionally teenagers are discourteous because they suppose it might be a way to impress others, or because they've seen their musketeers bear this way.No matter how grumpy or cross your child gets, your child still values time talking and connecting with you. You just might need to be a little further understanding if your child is short-tempered or changeable. It can help to a flashback that this phase will generally pass.

Handling discourteous behavior

Ways to handle discourteous behavior includes: communication, connections, and discipline

Tips for communication

1. Stay calm. This is important if your child reacts with an attitude to a discussion. Stop, take a deep breath, and continue calmly with what you wanted to say.
2. Use humor. A participated laugh can break a stalemate, bring a new perspective, lighten the tone, and take the heat out of a situation. Just avoid putting your child down or being sardonic.
3. Ignore shrugs, raised eyes, and wearied aesthetics if your child is generally carrying the way you want.
4. Check your understanding: occasionally teenagers are discourteous without meaning to be rude. You could say something-like, that comment came across as enough obnoxious. Did you mean to behave rudely?
5. Give descriptive praise when your child communicates positively.

Tips for connections

Be a role model. When you're with your child, try to speak and act the way you want your child to speak and act towards you. For example, if you swear a lot, your child might find it hard to understand why it's not OK for them to swear.

Still, another trusted grown-up might be suitable to support your child, If there's a lot of pressure between you and your child. This can ease the strain.

Check-in with your child to make sure there's nothing that's making your child feel particularly stressed or bothered.

Tips for discipline
1.   Set clear family rules about behavior and communication. For illustration, you could say, we speak hypocritically in our family. This means we don't call people names. It's a good idea to involve your child in conversations about the rules.
2.   Focus on your child's behavior and how you feel about it. Avoid any commentary about your child's personality or character. Rather than saying, You're rude, try saying, I feel hurt when you speak like that to me.
3.   Talk about, set, and use consequences, but try not to set too numerous. At times, it might be applicable to use consequences for effects like rudeness, swearing, or name-calling.

Things to avoid teenage discourteousness

Arguing infrequently works for parents or teenagers. When we get angry, we can say things we don't mean. A further effective approach is to give yourself and your child some time to calm down. It'll be hard to calmly bandy what you anticipate of your child if you're angry or in the middle of an argument. A further effective approach is to tell your child that you want to talk and agree on a time for a discussion.

Being a guard is veritably infrequently useful. Try not to take things personally. It might help to remind yourself that your child is growing up and trying to assert their independence. Indeed though you have further life experience, speaking to your child about how to behave is likely to turn them off listening. However, you might need to spend time laboriously harkening to your child first, If you want your child to hear you.

Troubling isn't likely to be an important thing. It might increase your frustration, and your child will presumably just switch off. Sarcasm will nearly clearly produce resentment and increase the distance between you and your child.

It might be a warning sign that there's a deeper problem, If your child's station towards you and your family does not respond to any of the strategies suggested above.You might also be concerned if your child:

1.	Show signs of depression like feeling sad, tearful, temperamental or perverse, or withdrawing from family, musketeers or usual conditioning
2.	Runs down from home or stops going to academy regularly
3.	Uses physical or verbal violence towards other family members.

It's OK to seek help and advice, If you're concerned about your child's behaviour.Here are some things you can do:
1.	Seek professional support – good people to talk to include academy counselors, preceptors, and your GP.
2.	Bandy the issue as a family, and try to work out ways of supporting each other.
3.	Talk to other parents and find out what they do.
4.	It's important to look after yourself too. However, you'll be better suitable to meet your child's needs, if you're managing your stress and meeting your requirements. Friends and family can be a great source of support, as can parents of other teenagers.

Chapter 3: Communicating effectively with teenagers

Good communication isn't the first term that's inescapably associated with teenagers! Slammed doors, crying, murmuring and arguments are maybe more the norm. But because of this, rather than the malignancy of it, it's important to suppose hard about how you communicate with teenagers. Of course, there may be specific motifs that spring to mind when agitating communicating with teenagers. Examples include coitus, medicines, and alcohol. It is, still, nearly more important to suppose about keeping communication going when you aren't concerned about specific issues on a day-to-day basis. Communicating about big things will be much easier, if you can achieve this.

Ten Tips for Communicating with the Teenagers

1. Give them openings
Rather than sit your teenager down for a formal talk, it's better to keep communication channels open all the time. Encourage them to help you prepare food, and converse as you do so, or make sure that you give them a lift to an exertion once a week, to give you a bit of time to talk without pressure. Family mealtimes are also a good way to make sure that everyone is coming together to converse on a regular basis.
2. Hear
We all like to be heeded, but numerous of us don't take time to hear from others. Take time to hear what they're saying, and look at their body If your teen wants to talk. Give them your full attention and it'll pay tips
3. Ask why, but don't make judgments
Pointing out that a particular piece of behavior was stupid isn't the stylish launch to a discussion. Rather, it's stylish to assume that your teen had a reason for their conduct, and ask them about it. It's important to keep an open mind about why they made that choice and try to understand their thinking process. Try to avoid making

any judgments about them, and this will help them to avoid judging others.

4. Don't assume or charge

Just as with young children, it's important not to assume that you know what's going on, or what has happened. In particular, don't ask leading questions. Rather, ask general questions similar as Will you tell me what's been passing? or I'm bothered that you haven't been quite your usual tone. Is everything OK?

5. Be there to help

All through their lives, you have been there to help, whether they're having trouble with schoolwork, difficulties at the academy, or with musketeers. Why would you stop now? Indeed though they're trying to establish their own identity, teenagers need to know that you're still there. Use questions similar to: Can I do anything to help? or Is there anything that you would like me to do? These types of questions make it clear that you're letting them decide if they want you to be involved.

This is particularly important if they're telling you about commodities like bullying. They may be anxious about telling you because of your possible response, so you need to make sure that what you do is helpful. You might, for illustration, say What I'd like to do is , do you suppose that would help?

6. Don't just tell, let them think things through

Most of us will presumably honor that we learn a whole lot more by making our miscalculations, and allowing effects through for ourselves than we do from being told what to do by someone different. Teenagers are the same. It's important, as the parent of a teenager, to have the confidence in them to believe that they can find the results of their problems. Your part is to help them to suppose effects so that they can do that. This may be with you, or by them, but it's important that you give them the space to do so, and make clear that you're available for discussion if necessary.

A veritably good way to make sure that you're enabling others to suppose effects for themselves is to make sure that you ask open-concluded questions(that is, questions that don't have a yes/ no answer). These frequently start with How ...?, What ....? or Why ...? It's also really important to remind them that you have confidence that they can do it. Don't assume that they know you do, take time to tell them. It's indeed stronger if you can tell them why. For illustration: I know you can do this because I've seen you do it before, I've every confidence that you can resolve this.

7. Do as I do, not just as I say

You're still a part model for your children. Your children have been watching and copying what you do for a time by the time they become teenagers. Still, including not smoking or not drinking redundant, you need to make sure that your behavior is applicable too If you want them to bear well. It isn't enough just to tell them.

8. Pick your battles

Some things are more important than others. Pick your battles so that you win the ones that matter, and let the others go. Still, your teen is less likely to be suitable to distinguish when you're seriously critical, as opposed to just a bit lukewarm If all you do is denounce. rather, try to be positive about the commodity if you don't like the briefness of the skirt, perhaps praise its color or the way that she has done her make-up.

9. Don't react to anger with anger or hurt

Flashback, you're the grown-up. As our runner on managing with Teenagers makes clear, it's important to flashback this, and to model the behavior that you want to see. It's hard to stay calm, but it's vital to do so. Still, take yourself down, explaining why you're doing so, If necessary. Return to the discussion later, when you're calm.

It's also important to flashback that your teenager doesn't mean I detest you, you've ruined my life! What they mean is that they're worried, and you're there and can be cried at. It may sound like it, but it's not particular, and you need to make sure that you don't take it that way.

10. Avoid asking too numerous delicate questions

You don't want your teen to lie to you. Immaculately, you would like them to feel suitable to talk to you about anything. But that may not be the case, especially if they're doing a commodity that they know you suppose is wrong, or indeed actually illegal.

It's thus better to avoid asking straight questions about delicate subjects unless you're set for them to lie or avoid the question. Just keep asking open questions and keep the communication channels open. Hopefully, they will also come to you when they want to talk. Occasionally questions are necessary. You may find that there are times when you need to ask delicate questions. However, for illustration, you find medicines or medicine-taking outfits in your teenager's room, If. In that case, it's better to take a straight approach, indeed though you still need to avoid making judgments. Keep your approach as neutral as possible, and just ask them to talk to you about it. Use expressions like, Please tell me what's happening. I'd like to know further about this.

Remember, your teenager is a person, growing into a grown-up. They're no longer small children and are likely to be abnormally sensitive about that. It's important to admire them and show that you do so, by giving them time and space to communicate with you. The more you push your kiddies, the further they get protective and dig in their heels. They come reactive in the form of a trap or shutting down and ignoring you. When they aren't exploding, they're allowing the following: My parents don't have an indication, so what's the point of trying to explain myself? I'll just tune them out.

Clamming up or exploding are both ways teenager's attempt to manage their stress and defend themselves. These may be the only ways your teen knows how to communicate when the effects get violent — which of course only causes further conflict.

5 helpful secret for communicating with kids through the delicate adolescent years

1. Start with Understanding, Indeed When You Don't Understand
Here's a simple secret that will help you in everything you do with your teen. No matter how hard it might be, try to start all relations with your child with understanding, indeed if you don't completely agree or indeed relatively comprehend what they're talking about.
Here is an illustration. You find your child online drooling with her musketeers when she's supposed to be doing her practice. It drives you crazy because you're thinking, She's slightly getting by in the academy and she doesn't feel like watching or understand that she needs to do her schoolwork. Your teen, on the other hand, is allowing me to get online and talk with Skyler. However, all the

other girls will be against me, If we don't put on makeup after the fight we had in the hall moment.

You and your child are living in two different realities. Ask your child why she's drooling. Try to be understanding of her reality, indeed if you don't fully get it. Once you know what's going on, try saying: I understand how delicate it's for you when you fight with one of your musketeers. I also know that you need to pass this test hereafter. Schoolwork is your job and it's your responsibility to do it to the stylish of your capacities. Let's sit down and suppose a good way you can manage your time tonight. Try not to say I understand, but … which will simply qualify what you've just said. Start from a place of understanding, and try to put yourself in your child's shoes first before telling her what needs to change.

2. Do not Get Emotional or Take It personal

Emotion is your adversary when you're trying to get through to your teen. Remind yourself that what he says and does isn't a reflection on you. You may not like how he's carrying — or indeed how he's thinking — but keep your feelings out of it, even if his behavior impacts you. I'm not saying this is an easy thing to do. It's tough, but it's very, very effective, and is a skill you can learn just like any other. I tell parents to repeat this mantra to themselves before talking to their kiddies

This is just the job of parenthood. It's not personal. When you think about it, there's no reason to be frenetic at your child for being himself. He may be making a poor choice, but the variety is that he might not yet have the skill set to make a better one. So your job is to help guide him to more choices so he can, in turn, develop better problem-working skills.

Try to just concentrate on your job as a parent; it'll help you be less emotional. When you feel frustrated, flash back , do not take it personal. Originally, your child's habits are like yours when you set boundaries. Tell yourself that this is simply a problem to break and part of the parenthood business as usual.

3. Ask Honest Questions … Not Loaded Questions

Ask your teen for his ideas and be cooperative. Let him see that you believe in him and that you're not frenetic at him for floundering in his life. When you let him see that you have faith in his capacities and he has the space to work things out on his own, you'll begin to develop true confidence in him. Don't ask loaded questions that put your child on the guard. Are questions similar: why can't you get up on time? What's wrong with you? Just leads to conflict, not result. Rather, try opening a discussion with:

Eli, do you have any ideas for how you might get up on time?

Still, offer many of your own and ask which one would work for him, if he says he doesn't know. Let your teen know that his problems are his to break. Don't step into his box. Give him the occasion — yes, occasion — to break his own problems.

But, be sure to let him know that you're there to help him figure out results, to consult with him. Oh, and be sure to let him deal with the natural consequences of his actions. Retaining the problem means retaining the consequences. Your ultimate thing is to help your child suppose for himself. Allowing for himself will, in turn, help him feel like he has some control over his world. Hear openly what he says and ask him to suppose critically about each choice. What will work and what will be problematic about each decision? What would be the natural consequences of each choice, and how would he feel about dealing with that?

4. Don't need your Child's Good Behavior

Don't feel, or show, as if you need your teen's cooperation, confirmation, or good behavior. As soon as you need something from your child so that you can feel better, you have put yourself in a vulnerable position because he doesn't have to give it to you. When you need something and don't get it, you'll naturally try harder by controlling and manipulating further. And your teen will come more and more recalcitrant or passively biddable — neither of which is good.

The truth is that you don't need anyone differently to prop you up. You can validate yourself and break your problems. So if your child is acting out, that's his problem. Your problem is to decide how you'll choose to bear toward him. That's in your hands, not his. Ask yourself, how do I want to act, no matter how he's acting? What can I put up with and what can I? Take back your power and say to yourself, if my child is screaming at me, rather than demanding him to stop, I can turn around and walk down and not engage.

Let your child know you used to talk with him until he can approach you with civility. Here's the variety: when you aren't trying to get your child to change or shape up, you'll be suitable to make better choices for yourself. And your child will be less recalcitrant because he'll have no one to repel. When you're not trying to control him and you're not replying to him, he'll have to scuffle with himself rather than with you.

5. Don't do anything until you're Both Calm

Another rule of thumb is to avoid doing anything until you and your child have both calmed down. The fact is, you don't have to respond to your child when you're worried or when your child is worried and in your face. You can say nothing. You can take many twinkles or further if you need to.When feelings have evened out, you can sit down and talk with him. It's no good to try to bring up a delicate subject or resolve a conflict in the heat of the moment. So if either you or your child is worried, pause and come back when you can address the effects more calmly.Still, that's when you have to hold on to yourself and make sure you don't get dragged into a fight, if you attempt a conversation with your child and he's rude or out of line. If your relationship with your child is currently such that it's impossible to have an open, respectful conversation, remember that it's still your job to stay firmly planted.

Have a watchword that you say to yourself like, I'm not going there no matter what. However, over time the baiting and enmity should calm down If you can do that constantly. This is called self-teaching and it works. And don't feel poorly if you get pulled back into a fight sometimes — staying strong isn't easy. The good news is that the more you refuse to engage, the easier it'll get to stay calm.

How to Establish good communication with your adolescent

Good communication with your teenager is one of the foundations of good parenthood. It's indeed more important in stressful situations, similar to what your family is going through. As children become adolescents, they typically get more involved with peers and talk less to parents. lower communication with parents can be a normal part of establishing independence. Teenagers still want and need to communicate with their parents, feel close to their parents, and be suitable to turn to their parents when they've problems or when they need to talk. Here are some tips for how to establish good communication with your teenager.

Listen

Listening is the single stylish thing you can do to establish good communication. Listening sounds simple but frequently isn't. Let your teenager finish his studies. Let him tell the whole story. Don't try to incontinently fix the situation. Remember that listening doesn't inescapably mean agreeing with everything he says. Occasionally he just needs to talk and know that you watch enough to try to understand. You don't have to intrude, agree or differ, or come up with an immediate result to his problems. For starters, you just have to hear.

Some simple listening rules:
 Pay Attention

Try to concentrate on what your teen is saying, rather than allowing about what you want to say back. Stop what you're doing, if you need to, to pay attention. Get rid of distractions so that you can hear well.

 Repeat from Time to Time.

Occasionally you can translate things your teenager has said to make sure you've got it right. This helps you understand, and also shows that you're listening. Be careful not to jump to conclusions when you repeat. For illustration, if your teenager says, I forgot to call my exploration officer history. I don't know why I've to call in every week. I'm doing fine. That's a stupid rule.

Show good listening similar to, you wonder why you have to call in when you're doing fine, right? Or Sounds like it's hard to flash back to call Mr. Johnson when you're doing okay, right? Examples of poor listening (jumping to conclusions) so, you want to break the rules again, right? Or, you know you have to call Mr. Johnson every week, so just go do it right now.

Ask Questions Sometimes

Asking occasional questions shows you're harkening and interested. Be careful not to ask too numerous questions or to take over the discussion with questions. In the illustration above, you might ask, what did Mr. Johnson say when you talked to him last week? or What if you gave him a call?

Listen Non Judgemental

When your teenager is talking to you about a concern or a problem, try not to judge or condemn him while you're in listening mode. Listen first. Hold your opinions until later, after your adolescence has finished.

Be Understanding

Show that you're trying to understand how your teen feels. Indeed if you don't inescapably agree with what your teenager is saying, it's still helpful to put yourself in your teen's shoes and communicate that you understand how he or she feels. Use Door Openers Rather Than Door Closers in Communicating.

Door Openers – Encourages your teen to talk openly. Tell me what happened. What do you suppose is the right thing to do? How do you feel about that? What happens next? That's a good question.

Door Closers – This makes your teen reluctant to open up.I don't want to hear that kind of talk. So what? I'll tell you what you ought to do … Why are you asking me? Don't come crying to me if you end up in a mess.

Other Communication Pointers

Communicate in Specifics

Teenagers need specifics, especially when it comes to communicating about rules and prospects. When giving your teenager instructions or feedback, talk about specific actions, not personalities or generalities. Also, whenever possible, tell the teen what to do, rather than just what not to do.

Talk About Behavior, Not particular Traits

For illustration, if your teenager has failed to do his chores you might say, you haven't finished your chores; I want you to get them done, rather than, You think you're too old to do chores? or If you weren't so reckless, I wouldn't have to remind you.

Talk About Specifics, Not Generalities

For illustration, it's better to say, Last week, you weren't ready to leave to go to treatment on time, rather of You're no way on time when we've to leave to go to treatment; you mess around every week.

Take a Break When things Get Heated

Parent – teenager arguments are a normal part of raising children. It's typical to periodically differ or have conflicts with your teenager. Occasionally you can tell that you or your adolescent is getting very angry or frustrated. As a grown-up, it's your responsibility to know when things are getting too heated and to take applicable action. You may notice yourself getting angry and raising your voice, or you may notice your teenager getting angry or heated. When this happens try some of the following responses. Stop and take a break from the disagreement, and let the effects cool down. You can always say, I want to take some time and think about this before we talk anymore. Your teenager may try to keep arguing, but just let it go for now.

Learn When It's Time to Stop.

The time to stop is before things have escalated to the point that people are saying or doing things that they will lament. Learn where this point is with your teenager. Learn where this point is with yourself — and stop the discussion before it's too late. However, If your teenager calls for a break first, respect that. Come back to the issue later, when Things have settled down. Once you start the break, be patient. Ordering your teenager to calm down will rarely get him to calm down; in fact, it may boomerang. It may take time for him to accept the need for a break in the discussion. Flashback, strong wrathfulness reduces on their own with time. Things will cool down. The disagreement may still be there, and that's normal. Nothing stays angry permanently. Occasionally physical exertion similar to walking, running, and exercising, can help reduce the intensity of the wrathfulness. Remember, getting your wrathfulness out often makes effects worse, not better. People infrequently get anything settled by yelling, screaming, name-calling, or violence. It's ok to feel angry, it isn't ok to act out on anger in dangerous ways. In times past, people allowed that it was healthy to let negative passions out toward other people similar to yelling and hitting objects. This approach, still, is frequently not helpful and can harm your relationship in the long run. Return to the discussion content after everyone has calmed down. Taking a break should not be used to avoid important motifs. Rather the break is designed to cool everyone down so when you return to communicating, better opinions can be made.

Be Ready to Communicate Openly When You Least Anticipate It.
You can't always predict when your teenager will want to talk to you. It infrequently occurs when the parent tries to push. However, you may get a response of I don't know, or Who cares? At other times, If you push it. The key is to be ready to use good communication skills when these times do. Making time for positive conditioning with your teenager can increase the liability of your teen communicating with you. For illustration, going fishing, cooking a mess, or going grocery shopping together provides openings for communication.

Give your adolescent a hug every day and tell them that you love them.
This is the first step in starting good communication. This will let them know that you support them and watch about them.
Talking with Your Adolescent about sex, Fornication, and connections
While it's important to understand colorful aspects of your teen's illegal sexual behavior, it's inversely important to have good communication with him about coitus and fornication in general. Accurate information about sexual behavior and open communication on the content is important for all teenagers, that is, youth who have and youth who haven't had illegal sexual behaviour. Communication that's in line with and supports your values is inversely critical. Studies have shown that utmost American teenagers learn further about sex and fornication from peers and from the media than from their parents. Studies also show that teens would like to be suitable to talk with their parents about sexual

topics. Being suitable to give good information and to communicate appropriately on sexual topics is helpful to all families, especially those in which sexual behavior has been problematic.

Basics about sexual development in aged children and adolescents.

At about 10 years of age, children begin to witness changes in their bodies known as puberty. They grow high and begin to gain weight, and their sexual organs begin to develop and enlarge. As they enter adolescence, other changes do, including bone and penis development, period, growth of pubic and facial hair, and changes in hormones. The changes in hormones affect adolescent sexual interests, studies, and actions.

Most teens know about sexual intercourse, contraception, and sexually transmitted infections (STIs). Still, they frequently have lots of misinformation, similar to allowing birth control capsules to help STIs. Some teens share in health education programs through their seminaries. Research has shown that these teens are more informed than those who gain information from the media or other adolescents. Participation in sex education programs results in:

a.   teens delaying the onset of sexual intercourse

b.   having lower frequent coitus

c.   Adding the use of contraceptives when they come sexually active

d.   having fewer sexual mates.

Studies show that — whether parents like it or not — the maturity of US adolescents are engaging in some form of behavior during their teenage times. Still, the rates of sexual exertion by teens have dropped in the last two decades. It's normal for teens to explore and experiment with sexual behavior. It isn't unusual for this trial with sexual behavior to include same-sex peers, regardless of sexual exposure.

Although adolescents can describe the pitfalls involved with sexual exertion, similar to STIs or gestation, they infrequently suppose that these problems will affect them. They don't know that about 25 percent of their sexually active peers have contracted an STI. Some STIs, similar to herpes and AIDS, have no given cure.

Given your son or daughter's history of illegal sexual behavior, you need to stress that normal and legal sexual behavior involves exertion between peers that are easily grounded on concurrence.

Consent means that 1) both actors agree to the behavior, 2) there's no force, pressure, or violence, and 3) the actors are of legal age and ability to give concurrence.

The age of consent varies from state to state and can be relatively complicated to interpret rightly in some countries. This is a good question to bandy and clarify with your teen's attorney. Many parents are uncomfortable talking with their children about sex. They suppose that teenagers shouldn't be having coitus and that talking about sex gives the wrong communication.

Some believe that sex should only take place within a marriage. But the reality in our society is that numerous teens are sexually active. They're being bombarded with dispatches about sex and fornication from their peers and the media. Given this reality, it's important for parents to openly discuss sex, fornication, and relationship opinions with their children as applicable to each child's position of understanding and to frame these conversations within their own beliefs and values. Parents must help their children acquire accurate information and form healthy values and stations about sexual behaviour.

Chapter 4: Parenting

Parents play a vital part in their children's life. They're the pillars of support, guidance, and love. Family is where life begins and love in no way ends. No matter how old a child gets there's nothing further comforting and soothing than their parent's arms. The part of parents in a child's life is beyond the idea of egging.

Parenthood takes action long before a child's birth and ultimately parents come to their children alter pride and vice-versa. There's nothing like them who can shape and mold a child's behavior and development. So parents should no way seize to inspire and help their children and thereby parents should strive to be the stylish schoolteacher in their child's life.

Maintaining a good Parent-Child relationship is the first step toward wise parenthood. Right from the birth of their seed, parents should be apprehensive of the enormous trustability and responsibility in their child's life. Not giving the proper guidance and love can seriously affect a child's life and can have serious impacts that will lead to character blights.The parent is the child's first schoolteacher and will remain a harmonious tutor in a child's life.

5 Mistakes parents make with teens and tweens

Your child is not a little kid anymore. They are a teen or a tween-- and it's time to tweak your parenthood skills to keep up with them. Yes, they are presumably more temperamental now than when they were youthful. And you have new effects to suppose about, like curfews, courting, new motorists, and musketeers who make you raise your eyebrows. Your teen or tween will test your limits and your tolerance, no doubt about it. But they are still your child. And, though they will not admit it, they still need you!

1.Expecting the Worst

Teenagers get a bad rap, says Richard Lerner, Ph.D., director of the Institute for Applied Research in Youth Development at Tufts University. Many parents approach raising teenagers as a fire, believing they can only watch helplessly as their sweet children transfigure into changeable monsters. But that sets you-- and your teen-- up for several unhappy, unsatisfying times together. The communication we give teenagers is that they're only good they're not doing bad things, similar as doing medicines, hanging around with the wrong crowd, or having sex. Negative prospects can promote the behavior you fear most. A Wake Forest University study showed that teens whose parents anticipated them to get involved in parlous actions reported advanced situations of these actions one time later. Focus on your child's interests and pursuits, indeed if you don't understand them. You could open a new path of communication, reconnect with the child you love, and learn something new.

2. Reading too many Parenthood Books

Rather than trusting their instincts, numerous parents turn to outside experts for advice on how to raise teens. Parents can tie themselves into knots trying to follow the advice they read in books, says Robert Evans, EdD, author of Family Matters How Seminaries Can manage with the Crisis in Child Rearing. It's not that parenthood books are bad.

 Books become a problem when parents use them to replace their ingrained chops. However, parents wind up more anxious and less confident with their children, If the recommendations and their particular styles don't fit. Use books to get perspective on confusing behavior and also put the book down and trust that you've learned what you need to learn. Get clear about what matters most to you and your family.

3. Sweating the Small Stuff

 Perhaps you do not like your tween son's hairstyle or choice of clothes. Or maybe they did not get the part in the play you know they earn. But before you stop by, look at the big picture. Still, give them the latitude to make age-applicable opinions and learn from the consequences of their choices, if it's not putting your child at threat. A lot of parents do not want growing up to involve any pain, disappointment, or failure, Evans says. But guarding your child against the realities of life takes down precious literacy openings-- before they are out on their own. Of course, you will still be there for guidance and comfort-- you are still the parent. But challenge yourself to step back and let your child know you are there for them.

4. Ignoring the Big Stuff

Still, alcohol, or other medicines, If you suspect your child is using tobacco(in any form). Indeed if it's" just" a cigarette or vaping, or alcohol or marijuana-- or indeed if it reminds you of your youth-- you must take action now, before it becomes a bigger problem. The times when kiddies are between 13 and 18 years old are an essential time for parents to stay involved, says Amelia M. Arria, Ph.D. She's the director of the University of Maryland's Center on Young Adult Health and Development. Parents might consider teen drinking a ritual of passage because they drank when they were that age. But the stakes are advanced now, Arria says.Watch for unexplained changes in your teen behavior, appearance, academic performance, and musketeers. And flashback, it's not just lawless medicines that are abused now-- traditional medicines and indeed cough drugs and ménage products are also in the blend.Still, if bottles of the drug go missing from your press, or if you find strange capsules, If you find empty cough drug packaging in your child's trash or pack. Take these signs seriously and get involved. guard all the drugs you have Know which products are in your home and how important the drug is in each package or bottle.

5. Too important, or Too Little, Discipline

Some parents, seeing a loss of control over their teens' behavior, crack down every time their child steps out of line. Others avoid all conflict for fear their teens will push them down. You do not have to do either of those effects. It's about changing a balance between obedience and freedom. Still, you may be suitable to make your teen or tween fall into line-- but at what price? Teens raised in rigid surroundings miss out on the chance to develop problems- working or leadership chops-- because you are making the opinions for them, If you put a too important emphasis on obedience. Yet too little discipline does not help, moreover. Teens and tweens need clear structure and rules to live by as they start to explore the world outdoors. As their parents, it's over to you to set your family's core values and communicate them through your words and conduct. That is being an authoritative parent, an approach that" helps children develop the chops they need to govern themselves in applicable ways," Lerner says.

Flashback, your influence runs deeper than you may suppose. Most teens say they want to spend more time with their parents. Keep making time for your child throughout the tween and teen times. Indeed when it doesn't show, you give the solid ground they know they can always come home to.

Parenthood can be the most satisfying work of adult life. Nothing brings further joy and pride than a happy, productive, and loving child. Each age and stage of a child's development has specific pretensions and tasks. For babies, it's to eat, sleep, and explore their world. For adolescents, it's to come to their person with their group of musketeers. Adolescents need numerous skills to successfully achieve their thing of increased independence. Some adolescents don't make this transition easily. Their movement toward independence can beget stress and grief for parents and families. Some aspects of this rough transition are normal and, while stressful, shouldn't alarm parents.

Starting beforehand is a stylish way for parents to prepare for their child's adolescence. The following are ways that parents can prepare themselves and their child for a smoother transition and lesser success in achieving the tasks of adolescent development:
a.   Providing a stable, safe, and loving home environment
b.   Creating an atmosphere of honesty, collective trust, and respect
c.   Creating a culture of open communication at family mess times
d.   Allowing age-applicable independence and fierceness
e.   Developing a relationship that encourages your child to talk to you
f.   Tutoring responsibility for their things and yours
g.   Tutoring the significance of accepting limits
h.   Tutoring the significance of allowing before acting
 These are complex processes that do gradationally and start during immaturity. A teenager's adolescent times will be less stressful when parents and child have worked together on these tasks throughout the child's earlier development. The capability to talk openly about problems is one of the most important aspects of the parent and child relationship. Developing this relationship and open communication takes time, continuity, and understanding. The relationship develops gradually by spending time with the teen. One challenge is sharing quality, not rushed time for parents to spend with their adolescents; as schedules with afterschool conditioning, sports and jobs come busy during adolescence. Family mess times, participating stories of parents' adolescence, playing board games, jaunts, recesses, and fests are important openings for parents to spend time with their adolescents. Parents should also try to spend some individual time with each child, praising positive actions and talking about delicate or disturbing effects. This relationship creates the foundation for talking with the child when struggles and conflicts crop during adolescence.

A parent-child relationship that is veritably stressful or worried during the preadolescent times can be a strong signal that professional help may be demanded. Parents' investment of time and energy in the child's early times can help small problems of childhood from getting larger problems of adolescence.

The role of Parents in a Child's life

• To develop skills
Parenthood is a no way - ending skill. Once you subscribe to it there's no looking back. You'll have to take charge and make the utmost of your time. Parenthood and child development are in a symbiotic relationship. When one flourishes, the other automatically finds balance. And this is the introductory rule of every parent-child relationship.
Parents contribute to the cognitive, socio-artistic, physical, internal, and spiritual development of an existent. Maternal values and moxie play a vital part in the healthy parenting of a child in all these areas.

• The foundation of all beliefs
The profile of cognitive capacities, beliefs, ethical values, managing defenses, and salient emotional moods that characterize each child at each experimental stage is the result of different influences operating in complex ways. Most scholars of moral development agree that the most important determinants of the different biographies include the inherited physiologic patterns that are called temperamental rates, maternal practices and personality, quality of seminaries attended, connections with peers, the ordinal position in the family, and, eventually, the literal period in which late adolescent and early adolescence are spent. As children develop from babies to teens to grown-ups, they go through a series of experimental stages that are important to all aspects of their personhood including physical, intellectual, emotional, and social.

• Support and guidance
The proper part of the parent is to give stimulants, support, and access to conditioning that enable the child to master crucial experimental tasks. A child's learning and socialization are most told by their family since the family is the child's primary social group. Happy parents raise happy children. Child development lies its root in their parents. Nothing can overcome the severity of a child's parenting. A parent thereby acts as a visionary to their children. There's nothing worldly that comes near to the offerings of

parenting. What parents do for their children out of love will always have an unforgettable comment on the child's life.

A child who has no way to admit balanced parenting will continue to advance for the rest of their lives. Parents also play a major part in the tone- of confidence of their children. If you want to increase the tone- of confidence of your child.

• Providing a good life

Education is one of the milestones in a child's development. A good education will hand over a satisfying career to the person and thereby they can serve society and return its bounties. It's imperative to know how parents impact the lives of their seed and plays an important part in the child's physical, internal, fiscal, emotional, and career development

Chapter 5: Overparenting

Over parenting is another word for hovering and micromanaging. When parents do for their children what they can and ought to do for themselves, it's called over parenting. When they try to fix or help their children's miscalculations, it's over parenting. We also took a deeper look at two reasons utmost of us do this (to a lesser or lower extent) the race for council, and the fear of parlous and self-harming actions

Parents today feel like their kids can't be successful without them helping at every turn and swimming over them. They spend so important time planning, guarding, directing, and pecking that they're eventually suppressing their growth. We're taking away the capability for our children to learn self- efficacy, says Lythcott-Haims. This incredibly important skill is a fundamental aspect of the mortal psyche. It's when individuals realize that their conduct leads to issues and that they have the power to direct their own lives. However, they also need to do further thinking, and planning, If our children are to make self efficacy. We may ensure some short-term pretensions by over helping, but it comes as a long-term cost to their sense of tone. We should be more concerned that they have the habits, skill set, mindset, and heartiness to be successful no matter what their future holds. This is worrisome because we all want our children to be suitable to serve without us, to fulfill their dreams, and live happy, healthy, successful lives.

How overparenting affect children

The underlying fear is that children will make miscalculations, irrecoverable miscalculations. It's called catastrophizing, imagining the worst and projecting it way into the future, rather than dealing calmly with the issue at hand. When parents are too important and overprotective, the kids hear the communication. I don't believe you can handle this yourself, so I've to do it for you. Eventually, the kiddies start to believe it, another important reason to stop over parenting.

From connections to academics, from chores to a job, this communication and belief cripple our children. They gradually stop thinking for themselves and stop solving. Why bother when Dad formerly knows the stylish way to do it and tells you so? They learn that they don't have to be responsible for themselves. Why pick your dirty clothes up off the bottom, when Mom can't tolerate it and will do it for you? Why take power for a problem in the academy, when your parents may intervene to reduce the consequences or shift the blame?

Another effect is that they become risk-avoidant. They don't take healthy pitfalls: an AP course that might be grueling and earn a B rather than an A, trying out for an exertion in which they do not formally exceed, indeed loading the dishwasher because it won't be done to a parent's anticipation. They avoid making any opinions because they might make the wrong decision.

1. You'd presumably admit that you learned the most from the failures and bummers in your life. Remember that most of them are not fatal. Give your child the gifts of disappointment and making miscalculations.
2. When your child does make a mistake, or you want to jump in to help one from passing, take a deep breath and ask yourself, whose problem is this? If it's your child's problem (and it frequently is), step back. However, let him handle it, if it's not about health or safety. He'll learn how able he is when he figures out how to fix it himself or assume responsibility for the consequences. You can be on the sidelines, available to help if he wants it.
3. Give your children age-applicable liabilities that include running a home. They need to know that life is about further than grades and the path to the council. It takes all members of a family to make home and family run easily … and they'll learn precious chops for living on their own.
4. Many opinions are not forever opinions. Today's choices can be traded in for another one hereafter. Let your kiddies know that while you anticipate them to take action to reach their pretensions, they always have choices.

How to avoid over parenting

Being a parent is one of the most delicate yet satisfying jobs on the earth. Having responsibility for the life of another may feel scary or inviting and may be causing you to over-parent your child. Over parenting frequently produces children who have a hard time making opinions on their own or living singly. You can avoid this by helping your child develop maturity, giving them some independence, helping them break, and dealing with your worries.

1. Recognise the warning signs. Look out for these issues which are frequently seen in children who are over parented: Meltdowns in response to minor challenges, incapability to entertain themselves for indeed a short time, asking for help incontinently without indeed trying to break a problem, expecting rewards or bribes to do anything, Constantly having to repeat yourself to your child, Feeling pressure to shield your child from failure or disappointment.

2. Avoid over praising your child. One mistake parents make is over praise their children for the most introductory accomplishment or task. This can beget your child to develop self-centered tendencies as they may come to believe that every single thing they do is major. While you should fete your child when they do well, taking care of introductory liabilities should infrequently be praised. Don't brag about your child's accomplishments to your musketeers or others. Share in a way that's non-showy.

3. Avoid over-censuring your child. Just as you shouldn't over praise your child, avoid exorbitantly censuring them as well. This will also beget your child to magnify the significance of their conduct if you're constantly reminding them of what they're doing wrong. Learn to pick your battles with your child and choose to correct them on the important effects. Let the small effects go. For case, if your child addresses back to a grown-up, this should always be corrected. Still, if you're constantly telling them to tuck their shirt in, consider letting that battle go at least temporarily.

4. Educate your child rather than doing everything for them. The adage goes that you can give a man a fish and he'll eat for a day, but if you educate a man to grope, he'll eat for a continuance. Borrow this doctrine with your children. conduct wisdom to them daily by talking your way through what you're doing while they're around.

After many times, see if they can do some of these effects on their own. Children learn with involved practice, not just through instruction and lectures. For instance, maybe you might show your child how to make an introductory mess like a sandwich if they're eight or aged. This can serve as a gateway to them understanding how to feed themselves and maybe indeed learning how to cook an introductory mess. You might also educate them about other effects like how to do their hair, how to clean up, or any other task that's useful and age-appropriate.

5. Hold them responsible for their mistakes. However, which children tend to do, hold them responsible for their conduct, if your child does mess up. This will prepare your child for the real world where miscalculations naturally lead to occasionally serious consequences. Set corrections that are fair, age applicable, and meaningful. It's also important to be calm and show some empathy when giving discipline so your wrathfulness itself does not come as the primary thing your kiddies are trying to avoid. For Instance, if your child has been picking on other kiddies at the academy because of their apparel, consider making them levy at a homeless sanctum or haze kitchen if they're old enough.

Encouraging Independence

1. Allow them to dress in the morning. One way you can begin helping your child develop independence is to allow them to dress themselves. This gives your child the space to express themselves and can also relieve you of the burden of having to choose their outfit each day. However, give them the option of two or three different outfits, and also allow them to choose. If your child is too youthful to choose their clothing. Set certain boundaries concerning the length and miserliness of the apparel. You might not allow films that you suppose are too short or see-through apparel.

2. Avoid setting strict routines. Give your child some inflexibility in their diurnal schedule, particularly if they're aged. Ultimately they should have the responsibility to get themselves up in the morning, and by the time they're aged, you should make sure you aren't still waking them up, especially not multiple times. Avoid subscribing

them up for too numerous after academy conditioning. Allow them to have free time so that they can develop as individuals and determine their interests. For instance you might bear that your children begin their schoolwork within thirty twinkles of arriving home but that any time after that can be used as they suppose to fit. Give your child some inflexibility with other effects like bedtime as well. Consider giving them a general thirty nanosecond period in which they must be in bed.

3. Give them chores. Allow your child to begin learning the significance of pitching in and doing their part by assigning their daily chores to complete. Assign them chores grounded on their age position. It's also important to decide what happens when they do not do their chores. Generally, boons should be earned by completing chores rather than giving discipline when they do not get done. Don't clean up your children's mess for them, especially if they're age five or over. Task them with keeping their room clean in addition to helping with general ménage chores like the dishes or the trash.

4. Avoid making all choices for them. In addition to their apparel and free time, allow your child to make certain choices for themselves. Maybe you're hoping that your child does soccer but they prefer to play softball. Allow them to play the sport of their choice. Allow your child inflexibility in other areas as well including their diet, choice of toys, or part-time job. (8) cover your kiddies from dire consequences, but allowing your kiddies to make less serious miscalculations that they should be suitable to handle can ameliorate their decision-making in the future.

5. Avoid over-giving your child. Spoiling your child is a sure fire way to over-parent them. Though you should always take care of your child and tend to their requirements, you don't have to give in to all of their wants. Allow them to earn the effects that you give to them. This doesn't mean that you make your child work for gifts, but that you award them when they're keeping up with their liabilities and chores. Don't continuously give gifts to your children if they aren't doing well in the academy or if they aren't taking care of the effects that you do give them.

6. Allow your child to help you. However, stay to see if your child offers to pick it up for you If you drop a commodity. Also, when you're carrying the groceries into your home, don't refuse help if

your child offers, indeed if you can carry everything alone. Allow your child to take some burdens off of you, indeed if they're slight.

7. Allow them to choose their musketeers. Though your child may have connected with a friend or two who you don't authorize, don't try to micromanage these friendships. Allow your child to choose who they want to be musketeers with and who they don't. Don't try to force musketeers on them or take musketeers down. You can set parameters, still. Set a curfew for your child. Disallow them from engaging in certain actions, indeed if their musketeers are doing it. You can also encourage your child to talk to you about their musketeers. Offer some advice grounded on your own experience, but do not try to tell them what to do.

Teaching Problem working skills

1. Help them communicate results. Your child may be floundering with something, but don't just break the problem for them. Help them begin to suppose ways that they can break the problem on their own, indeed if you formerly know a result. In case, if you're helping them with their schoolwork, and they got the wrong answer, do not point out their mistake. Encourage them to review the problem rather. Still, help and educate them, but allow them to fall many times under your supervision, If your child is learning to ride a bike without a training bus. It's frequently the miscalculations that children make that are the topmost preceptors and motivators to success.

2. Avoid bailing them out of certain situations. You may notice that your child frequently tries to quit effects once they come uncomfortable, but it's frequently in times of discomfort that growth occurs. Avoid coming to your child's delivery all of the time and allow them to figure out a way to manage on their own. For case, if your child wants to switch out of a class because they don't have any musketeers, encourage them to make musketeers rather and avoid helping them to get out of the class.

3. Don't replace or fix lost or broken particulars immediately. However, avoid fixing or replacing them, If your child constantly

breaks their phone or toys. This will educate your child that you won't save them each time they're careless. Encourage them to fix or replace the effects that they break, particularly if this is a regular circumstance. Children tend to watch more for effects that they had to work hard for. Consider allowing them to complete fresh chores for plutocrats so that they can ultimately replace their items.

4. Allow your child to resolve their issues with their peers. Avoid intermediating in arguments that your children might be having or in fights that your child might have with their musketeers. As long as these dissensions aren't physical, your child isn't in peril but is rather learning precious conflict resolution skills. Lead them by your illustration. Allow your child to see you resolve conflicts with your mate, family, and musketeers. Know when to step in. However, you should intermediate, if your child is being bullied by someone.

Handling Your Parenting Fears

1. Don't make your child the center of your life. Though you love your child veritably much, avoid making them the entire focus of your life. A child who grows up believing everything centers around themselves will have a lot of difficulties navigating real connections and dealing with conflicts of any kind. Learn to watch your own life as well. Devote yourself to your career, hang out with musketeers, spend time with your partner, and explore your other interests.

2. Make a plan. Maybe the importance of your solicitude or anxiety in parenthood with your children arises from not having a plan if commodity should go amiss. Maybe one of your worries is leaving your teenagers at home alone while you're at work. In this case, to assuage your solicitude, you can install a home alarm system so you know they will be defended while you're down. Still, get them a helmet and knee pads, If you're upset about your child falling while riding their bike.

3. Get spiritual or meditate. Getting in touch with your church is a great way to calm down any internal anxieties that you might be facing. Take some time each day to supplicate or meditate. Go to an

original place of deification. Connect with musketeers who are connected to their spiritual side.

4. Talk to other parents. One way to calm your fear is to talk to other parents who can help you keep your worries in check. Frequently, when we pass effects to others, we might realize how unrealistic and unsupported our worries are. Musketeers will be suitable to give you advice on how to let up on your children a bit and give them more independence.

5. Seek professional help. Seek out some fact-grounded papers specifically about your particular problem. However, talk to an internal health professional for guidance, If you still feel like you're in over your head after trying colorful approaches to an issue. Do not feel like you need to figure everything out all on your own.

6. Cover what you watch on television. The types of programs that you watch on TV may be directly impacting your parenthood style. Maybe you watch the nocturnal news each day or view other violent programming on the regular. exploration shows that the further violence you see on television, the more violently you'll interpret the world. Switch up your worldview by viewing more positive and tranquil programming.

7. Exercise self- care. In taking care of your child, don't forget to watch for yourself. Eat healthy foods. Exercise regularly. Plan one thing, no matter how small, per day that you can look forward to. Read a book, watch a film, or have a gym day.

CONCLUSION

In conclusion, the best way to raise an amazing teenager against all odds is:

Stop Making Everything about You

Many parents try to live with their children because they're unsatisfied with their adolescence. They may indeed relate to their child's grades and conditioning as ours. Learn to separate what's yours from what's theirs. We also have to stop trying to fester our kiddies into a commodity they're not. We'll each be much better off if we love our children for who they're and support them.

Educate Them on New skills

The only way our children will learn to do things for themselves is if we give openings for them to learn new skills. This starts during preschool when we ask our children to dress themselves and use a chopstick duly. With each new time, there are so numerous chances to help develop their skill set. The stylish way to educate teens on a new skill is to: 1) do it for them, 2) do it with them, 3) watch them do it on their own, and 4) let them do it on their own. Wouldn't you rather gradually educate your kiddies and not have to arm everything in the way to council move- in the day?!

Let Them fend For Themselves and Learn From Their miscalculations

It's so important that our children learn how to speak up for themselves and communicate with authority numbers and peers likewise. We've to stop trying to clean up all their messes for them and cover them from failure. The only way they will grow is if they make miscalculations and learn how to handle them.

Give your kiddies Experiences

Indeed if it's completely out of your comfort zone, try to let your kiddies witness conditioning without you that will help them make tone- confidence and independence. Sleepovers, each-day sports or other competitions, boarding passages, and sleepaway camps are some good examples. Last summer, my son went off to sleepaway camp for four weeks, and it was veritably delicate for me. I cried for days fussing about him. But, you know what? When I saw him on visiting day, I was blown down by how happy he was and how mature he acted. I was petrified that he'd pick over bad habits and come to a rotten sprat, but the contrary happened – he came to an indeed more amazing interpretation of himself.

By confirming some of our parenthood ways now, we can more prepare our kiddies for a successful life ahead of them.